Aha! Moments In
BRAND
Management

Aha! Moments In
BRAND
Management

Commonsense Insights to a
Stronger, Healthier Brand

Larry Checco

Order this book online at www.trafford.com
or email orders@trafford.com

Most Trafford titles are also available at major online book retailers.

Printed in the United States of America.

ISBN: 978-1-4269-9768-6 (sc)
ISBN: 978-1-4269-9769-3 (e)

Library of Congress Control Number: 2011917738

Trafford rev. 11/22/2011

 www.trafford.com

North America & international
toll-free: 1 888 232 4444 (USA & Canada)
phone: 250 383 6864 ♦ fax: 812 355 4082

Contents

In loving memory of my father,

Larry Checco, Sr.

"I Don't Do Campaigns!"

I once had someone ask me, *"Larry, would you be interested in helping us with our branding campaign?"*

I gently replied, *"No."*

"But I thought you were a branding consultant," she said, a bit confused.

"I am. But I don't do branding campaigns."

"Why not?"

"Because a campaign has a beginning, a middle and an end," I replied. *"A brand, on the other hand, reflects <u>how you conduct your business every moment of every day.</u>"*

"Aha!"

Preface

"We Are Sorry"

At just about the time this book went to press, Rupert Murdoch shut down his media conglomerate's 168-year-old tabloid, *News of the World,* one of the world's largest circulating English-language newspapers. This was the consequence of a phone-hacking scandal in which, over several years, *News of the World* employees allegedly hacked the phones of thousands of British citizens—from innocent crime victims to members of the Royal Family—and bribed police officers for information. The scandal started that proverbial snowball rolling down a mountain.

As of this writing, several high-ranking Murdoch employees already had resigned or been arrested, and other parts of the tycoon's multi-billion-dollar, worldwide *News Corp* media empire were beginning to feel the ripple effects of the scandal, forcing Mr. Murdoch to issue the following public statement:

We Are Sorry.

The News of the World was in the business of holding others to account. It failed when it came to itself.

We are sorry for the serious wrongdoing that occurred. We are deeply sorry for the hurt suffered by the individuals affected. We regret not acting faster to sort things out.

I realise that simply apologising is not enough.

Our business was founded on the idea that a free and open press should be a positive force in society. We need to live up to this . . .

Sincerely,

Rupert Murdoch

File this under the all-too-familiar category of too little, too late.

Murdoch's plight is an archetypical example of what happens when organizations—regardless of how large or powerful—fail to understand that their brands are less a product of their marketing, advertising, public relations and political and financial connections, but instead are rooted in the public's expectations of trustworthiness, honesty, integrity, ethical behavior and decency.

The Murdoch *News Corp* scandal is just the tip of the iceberg. Beneath the roiling seas of our private and public sector worlds are countless companies and organizations locked in the icy, cold grasp of poor management that results in tarnished brands—or worse!

Full disclosure

In full disclosure, this book in many ways is very personal. I wrote it as much out of frustration and disappointment as anything else.

I'm old enough, and have been in the communications business long enough, to have witnessed countless CEOs, executive directors, board members, politicians, and dare I say religious leaders and others make the same mindless mistakes—and even more frightening, bad conscious decisions—again and again, much to the detriment of the organizations they ostensibly are charged to lead, as well as the clients, customers and followers their organizations profess to serve.

But you don't have to be in my business to understand where I'm coming from.

How well did your investment portfolio fair when the tech stock bubble burst in 2000-2001, or after the more recent Great Recession? Yet, these events occurred at a time when our financial institutions were aggressively marketing rock-solid brand images of themselves and encouraging us to invest with confidence ...

> **These events occurred at a time when our financial institutions were aggressively marketing rock-solid brand images of themselves and encouraging us to invest with confidence ...**

Or how many times have you donated money to a nonprofit only later to learn that your money was used in ways you did not intend . . .

Or how secure and safe do you feel when government agencies fail to fulfill their obligations to, we, the people . . .

Or when politicians misrepresent the truth . . .

Or when religious leaders and their institutions violate your trust?

Just read your local newspapers or watch the news. After a while the stories begin to repeat themselves. Whether it's a company, financial institution, nonprofit organization, political party or politician, government agency or religious institution, it's the same old same old—lost trust, often due to poor leadership, lax ethical standards or just plain poor decision-making, resulting in a severely tarnished brand, or worst yet, an organization's total demise.

The irony here is that every one of these organizations, if asked, would say they would like nothing more than to earn your trust and respect. More ironic is that the vast majority of them spend an enormous amount of time, energy and financial resources trying to do just that.

In my first book, ***Branding for Success: A Roadmap for Raising the Visibility and Value of Your Nonprofit Organization***, I laid out an argument for why nonprofit organizations need to clearly define who they are, what they do, how they do it and—most important, why anyone should care.

The book also provided a roadmap for how organizations, regardless of their size or financial resources, could efficiently and cost-effectively go about defining, promoting and protecting their respective brands, or reputations.

Since 2005, when **Branding for Success** was first published, I've traveled around the country, done scores of speaking engagements and talked to thousands of people in the nonprofit and for-profit sectors, government agencies and other institutions.

During that time, I was fortunate enough to listen as well as talk, and what I learned is that when it comes to branding, lots of low-hanging fruit goes unpicked—or worse yet, unrecognized or unnoticed—by organizations and companies of all stripes and sizes.

> **When it comes to branding, lots of low-hanging fruit goes unpicked—or worse yet, unrecognized or unnoticed—by organizations and companies.**

You won't find the following pages filled with a lot of marketing babble or charts and graphs related to branding theories. Rather, they hold what I believe to be some fundamental, self-evident truths wrapped in common sense.

After many of my speaking engagements I've had people say to me, *"This isn't what I expected, but it's what I needed."* One executive director said to me, *"Larry, you're simply packaging the commonsense things many of us miss because we're so busy looking at the 'big picture'. This has been an 'Aha!' moment for me."*

This Book

This book is my attempt to identify as many *"Aha!"* moments as I can for you, the reader.

Most of what I advocate here are commonsense ideas and strategies that are relatively easy and inexpensive, or cost-free, to implement. Some, however, do require introspective, not-so-easy-to-make cultural shifts in the way your company or organization envisions itself and conducts its business. Others simply require paying greater attention to detail.

> **Most of what I advocate here are commonsense ideas and strategies that are relatively easy and inexpensive, or cost-free, to implement.**

It makes no difference whether your organization is a for-profit or not-for-profit, a government agency, political party, religious institution or local civic organization, large or small, richly or poorly endowed. The principles contained in ***Aha! Moments in Brand Management: Commonsense Insights to a Stronger, Healthier Brand*** are timeless and apply to you.

Like ***Branding for Success***, this is a relatively short, easy-to-read book. Experience tells me that busy people don't have the time to read academic tomes.

My hope, however, is that you will find this book insightful and useful as you go about the business of managing your brand on a daily basis. It's not so much a "*how-to*" guide as it is a "*we-need-to-give-this-more-thought*" book. That's why at the end of each chapter is a section titled "Let's give this some thought," which is meant to help initiate discussions at staff and board meetings.

> **It's not so much a "how-to" guide as it is a "we-need-to-give-this-more-thought" book.**

I feel I will have done my job if this book finds its way into the hands of one or two decision makers in a company, organization, institution or government agency who understand the value of stepping back and taking an honest, introspective, contemplative look at how management and an organization's brand are integrally related. I will feel even better if they act on some of what they read here.

> **It's awfully difficult to separate management performance from brand identity.**

The fact is it's awfully difficult to separate management performance from brand identity. Just ask Rupert Murdoch.

A Bit About Branding

> *"A brand for a company is like a reputation for a person. You earn reputation by trying to do hard things well."*
>
> Jeff Bezos, Founder, CEO
> Amazon.com

A Bit About Branding

So That We're All Talking About the Same Thing

I've been asked, "What are the industry standards for branding?"

Given my decades of experience in the business, I can honestly answer, "There are none."

Some folks think that branding is all about marketing, advertising and public relations. Others believe that all you need is to develop an attractive logo and catchy tagline and, voila, "we have our brand."

> **Some folks think that branding is all about marketing, advertising and public relations.**

Still others feel they've fulfilled their branding obligations by handing out tchotskes or favors—namely pens, refrigerator magnets, stress balls, tote bags and the like, imprinted with their company's logo—at conferences or other relevant venues.

Many are simply confused by the word "brand."

Think "Reputation"
If you can't get your arms around the words "brand" or "branding," replace them with the term "reputation management."

> **If you can't get your arms around the words "brand" or "branding," replace them with the term "reputation management."**

Remember back to your high school days, and how keenly aware you were of—and how hard you worked on—your reputation every day? That's a lot of what good branding is all about.

In fact, the most fundamental questions good brand managers should address are: *"As an organization, who are we? And what do others think of us?"* As a former teenager, do these questions sound vaguely familiar?

The fact is, everything, absolutely everything, your company says or does reflects upon its brand—from the marketing messages it sends out (are they accurate and true?) to the morale of its employees (how motivated are they to be good ambassadors for your brand and to speak well of the organization for which they work?) right down to typos in company documents (how much attention does this organization pay to details?).

> **Everything, absolutely everything, your company says or does reflects upon its brand.**

If life has taught me anything, it's to maintain perspective. Therefore, you will find in these pages what I hope you perceive as a dash of humor, a pinch of tongue-in-cheek, a dab of home-spun storytelling that rings true, a bit of frustration (every writer's bane), some honest thoughts, and dare I say a pearl of wisdom or two.

Finally, I've also learned that good things, including good brands or "reputations", take a long time to create and nurture before they gain faith and credence. The tragedy, as many of our once most venerated companies and institutions have learned recently, is that it takes very little time for all that trust and goodwill to unravel, often with dire consequences.

> **Good brands or "reputations", take a long time to create and nurture before they gain faith and credence.**

All the more reason to stay focused and vigilant when it comes to managing and safeguarding your brand.

Aha! Moment #1

Branding isn't Just About Trust— It's ALL About Trust!

"To be persuasive we must be believable; to be believable we must be credible; to be credible we must be truthful."

Edward R. Murrow
Broadcast Journalist

Branding isn't Just About Trust—
It's ALL About Trust!

What's Your Pattern?

I'm the father of two sons who are now in their twenties and turning into fine young men. When they were younger, however, I used to call them Butch and Sundance because they always tried to stay one step in front of the law—and that was me! There were days the testosterone sloshed up against the walls of our house and I thought my wife would be canonized in her own time for her saintly patience. Anyone who has raised rambunctious children can relate.

During those difficult formative years—between the ages of 14 and 18— my oldest, in particular, in an effort to provide cover for things he did that most adults would think dangerous and land him in serious trouble one day, liked to fabricate stories.

Of course, as his parents, my wife and I feared that his inability to tell the truth might lead him to make serious mistakes from which he would be unable to recover and which could possibly alter

> **The lying itself showed a lack of good sense because he was smart enough to know that sooner or later he was going to be found out.**

his life forever. But the lying itself showed a lack of good sense because he was smart enough to know that sooner or later he was going to be found out.

I'd say to him *"Son, you and I are going to have a tough time relating to each other because it's hard for me to maintain a relationship with someone I can't trust."* I also told him that people look at behavioral patterns when they assess others. *"That's because they don't have the time to re-evaluate you every time they come in contact with you, and if they determine that your pattern is to lie or deceive, even when you tell the truth their inclination is not to believe you."*

> **People look at behavioral patterns when they assess others.**

Well, the same holds true for companies, organizations and institutions.

Years later, my son told me his rationale for his adolescent storytelling was that it was much easier at the time to ask for forgiveness than it was for permission, which demonstrated his inexperience and adolescent perspective on life. Any company, organization, institution or public figure that has had to ask the public for forgiveness knows how humiliating it can be and the often-disastrous long-term reputational harm it can create.

> **Any company, organization, institution or public figure that has had to ask the public for forgiveness knows how humiliating it can be and the often-disastrous long-term reputational harm it can create.**

Aha!

The fact is: Your brand is your story, *NOT* your fairytale. It should be a true reflection of who you are and what you do, not who you'd like to be and what you'd like to do.

> **Your brand is your story, NOT your fairytale.**

In the long run it's a lot cheaper and far less humiliating to maintain a good, trustworthy reputation, or brand, than it is to try to catch up with one that has been tarnished in the public's eye, something I hope this book demonstrates in the pages that follow.

A Brand Screams Out TRUST ME . . .

. . . And a good brand always fulfills that pledge.

Companies spend an enormous amount of time, energy and resources to try to get us to trust that the products and services they sell are the best on the market or represent the best value for the price we pay . . . .

Financial institutions want us to invest with confidence . . . .

Nonprofits want us to trust that they are using our donations wisely and effectively . . . .

Political parties and politicians want us to believe that they are working in our, the public's, best interest rather than on behalf of special interest groups . . . .

Unfortunately, public skepticism and distrust of corporations, institutions and organizations of all kinds is at an all-time high. Trust, which many of us once unquestionably bestowed upon previously well-known and well-respected for-profit and nonprofit organizations, government agencies and many religious institutions—is now at an all-time low.

> **Public skepticism and distrust of corporations, institutions and organizations of all kinds is at an all-time high.**

Today, companies and organizations that _can_ demonstrate their trustworthiness over time—nay, live and breathe it every moment—are light-years ahead of many of their competitors.

You Need to Ask the Right Questions

As I travel around the country conducting workshops on organizational branding and leadership, I show a slide that I preface by saying, *"As simple as this slide appears, it's probably the most important slide I will show you today."*

The slide reads:

A good brand equals:

- *Trust*
- *Relationship building*
- *Cooperative, collaborative opportunities to advance your goals and objectives*

The dialogue that follows usually goes something like this:

"How many of you have developed strategic plans for your companies or organizations?" I ask. Most of the hands in the room go up.

"And when you're sitting around the conference table, what's the first question most people ask when it comes to strategic planning?"

Many reply with, *"What are the goals and objectives we want to achieve?"* Some phrase it differently, *"Where do we want to be three to five years from now?"* which is essentially the same question.

"And how do you plan to get there?" I ask.

Some reply, *"By increasing our marketing and advertising efforts to better reach our customers and clients."* Others say, *"By creating strategic alliances or relationships with other organizations."* Still others respond, *"Through downsizing our workforce,"* or *"restructuring our budget,"* or *"changing our board or executive leadership."*

Many, frankly, don't know how they're going to achieve their goals and objectives. *"That's why we're going through the process of creating a strategic plan; to determine how,"* I had one executive inform me, which I thought was a good, honest, straightforward answer.

I press on: *"For those of you who said 'by targeting our customers and clients' or 'creating relationships with others', how do you propose to do that?"*

Usually, there's a long pause.

I believe that in all the times I've been through this exercise, only one person saw where I was taking the conversation and said, *"By getting them to trust us."*

Aha!

> **Trust must be the rock-solid foundation upon which all of our endeavors are launched and relationships are based.**

And therein lies the rub. Most organizations are so focused on achieving their goals and objectives that they fail to see that trust must be the rock-solid foundation upon which all of our endeavors are launched and relationships are based.

Unfortunately, many organizations tacitly ignore the trust factor, or if they do acknowledge trust as one of their core values, tend to increasingly and insidiously ignore its relevance as they strive—shoulders to the grindstone, noses to the wheel—to get to where they want to be.

If, for example, increasing your bottom line or fundraising revenue streams is your organization's top strategic goal and that's all the organization is focused on, then false advertising, deceptive business practices, or turning a blind eye when others around you engage in unethical behavior may be some of the more tacit ways management allows for achieving goals and objectives.

In the short run, your organization may achieve its goal of increased profits or funding. But as many organizations have learned—and we've witnessed the demise of a lot of them over the past several years—these practices do not bode well for a company's or organization's long-term survivability.

In short, the first question every organization should ask when it comes to strategic planning is:

"What are we doing to earn—and keep—the trust of those, both inside and outside of our organization, that will enable us to form the kinds of relationships we need to achieve our goals and objectives? Moreover, what are we doing to create the kind of organizational culture and workplace environment that values, nurtures, encourages and allows trusting relationships to develop and flourish?"

Once you have the answers to those questions, your goals and objectives will follow.

"Let's give this some thought"

Questions to initiate and stimulate staff and board discussions

- Do the people we are trying to reach with our products, programs, services, etc.—namely our customers, clients and others—trust us?

- If so, do we know this to be a fact or is it simply a wishful assumption on our part?

- If not, what have we done <u>not</u> to earn, or to lose, their trust?

- What do we need to do to earn and keep their trust?

- Do we have the right people in the right positions who can accomplish this for us? If not, are we prepared to make the decisions necessary to ensure that we do have the right people in place?

- Are we doing everything in our power to create the kind of organizational culture and workplace environment that values, nurtures, encourages and allows trusting relationships to develop and flourish, both internally and externally?

- If not, what's holding us back?

- Is trust one of our core organizational values and, if it is, are we doing more than paying lip service to it?

Aha! Moment #2

Good Branding is Not About Marketing.
It's About Meeting Customer Expectations

> *"The golden rule for every businessman is to put yourself in your customer's place."*
>
> Orison Swett Marden
> Author, Founder of Success Magazine

Aha! Moment #2

Good Branding is Not About Marketing.
It's About Meeting Customer Expectations

Marketing and Branding are Not the Same

People often think that marketing and branding are one and the same. They believe that a well-orchestrated marketing and advertising campaign can, over time, instill brand trust and loyalty in whatever it is they are trying to sell.

The fact is marketing and advertising are strategies for selling products and services. Your brand is a reflection of everything associated with your organization, starting with the expectations you create. Brand trust and loyalty follow only when those expectations are met.

> Marketing and advertising are strategies for selling products and services. Your brand is a reflection of everything associated with your organization.

When Even Great Companies Get it Wrong

Propelled by a marketing effort the likes of which had never before been experienced by the American public, in 1958 the Ford Motor Company unveiled its "revolutionary" new vehicle, the Edsel.

Billed as the "Car of the Century," the Edsel boasted, among other things, innovations such as self-adjusting rear brakes, automatic lubrication, and something called a Tele-touch transmission, whereby the driver selected the gears by pushing buttons located on the center of the steering wheel.

The hype surrounding the introduction of Ford's new vehicle was unprecedented, and included a CBS television special called *The Edsel Show*, starring top entertainers of the day, including Bing Crosby, Frank Sinatra, Louis Armstrong, Bob Hope and Rosemary Clooney.

Riding the wave of this extraordinarily expensive media blitz, Ford had expectations of selling 200,000 Edsels in its first year on the market. It didn't quite work out that way.

Ford had expectations of selling 200,000 Edsels in its first year on the market. It didn't quite work out that way.

Sure, the pre-publicity Ford pumped into its new product immediately piqued people's interest and prompted curious Americans to flock to showrooms nationwide to get a gander of the future. But what they found fell far short of the expectations that Ford had managed to create through its own marketing and advertising efforts.

It turned out that once the product behind the curtain was revealed, Ford discovered that many automotive shoppers didn't like the Edsel's design, especially what became known as the car's "horse collar grill", nor the car's price. In addition, because the Tele-touch transmission, which was meant to be new and innovative, was placed in the middle of the steering wheel where drivers were accustomed to finding the car horn, it resulted in drivers inadvertently shifting gears.

Among many other engineering and design faux pas were quality control issues, with many Edsels actually leaving the Ford assembly lines unfinished. Uninstalled parts were placed in car trunks along with installation instructions for dealership mechanics. Even the hood ornament was at risk of vibrating off the car when it was driven at high speeds.

It didn't take long before the Edsel took on the acronym for "Every Day Something Else Leaks."

> **The Edsel took on the acronym for "Every Day Something Else Leaks."**

Time magazine, in a special issue titled The 50 Worst Cars of all Time, said of the Edsel, "It was kind of homely, fuel thirsty and too expensive." Regarding all the hoopla preceding the car's introduction into automotive showrooms, *Time* added, "It [the Edsel] was the first victim of Madison Avenue hyper-hype."

One Edsel aficionado probably stated it best when he wrote on his website: "The public thought there was something radically new coming out. But it [the Edsel] was really just another 1958 car. It had more gizmos and gadgets on it but it wasn't anything that lived up to the hype."

Even the largest and most aggressive marketing and media blitz up to that time couldn't save this woe-begotten experiment in automotive engineering and design from its fate. By November 1959, less than two years after being introduced to the public with great fanfare, Ford rolled its last Edsel off the production line.

Some estimate that Ford lost $250 million (nearly $2 billion in 2011 dollars). Other estimates go as high as $400 million when development costs are included.

Remember New Coke?

If you're too young to remember the Edsel marketing debacle, perhaps you're old enough to remember what happened to the Coca-Cola Company in 1985, when it launched New Coke. Failing to understand or meet its customers' expectations, New Coke turned into a brand manager's nightmare.

> **Failing to understand or meet its customers' expectations, New Coke turned into a brand manager's nightmare.**

Shortly after the launch, in Atlanta, where the Coke company is headquartered, people took to the streets in protest. Many original Coke lovers in communities around the country, fearful that the old Coke they so loved would no longer be available to them stocked their basements with the "real thing." Protest songs were written. The company phone bank was swamped with thousands of calls and consumer complaints.

It turned out that Coke company executives had totally underestimated and misunderstood the bond consumers felt toward their product and its fabled "secret formula".

To put an end to this marketing fiasco and consumer rebellion, 79 days after the launch of New Coke, the company returned to its original formula, now called Coca-Cola Classic®.

Aha!

It turns out that all the marketing dollars in the world—and who has more marketing dollars than Coca-Cola or the Ford Motor Company—cannot buy a desired brand. They learned the hard way that a truly good brand must meet or exceed customer expectations, not dictate them.

> **It turns out that all the marketing dollars in the world cannot buy a desired brand.**

Expectations Come in all Sizes

Unlike Ford or Coca-Cola, both of whom set the bars extraordinarily high for themselves, companies and organizations are far better off establishing expectations that they can at the very least meet, if not exceed.

> **Companies and organizations are far better off establishing expectations that they can at the very least meet, if not exceed.**

Coke actually launched New Coke to regain market share over its then top competitor, Pepsi. With the Edsel, Ford attempted—and failed—to make an epic statement about its ability to be at the cutting edge of automotive design and engineering. Both companies' brands suffered temporary setbacks as a result of these very expensive marketing ventures that ultimately ended in failure.

Not every company or organization, however, has the opportunity, resources or wherewithal to set such high expectations. Yet, every day most of us make promises—in effect, set expectations—that speak to the quality and trustworthiness of our brands.

> **Every day most of us make promises—in effect, set expectations—that speak to the quality and trustworthiness of our brands.**

And most often the consequences of not meeting those expectations are not readily visible to the company or organization, yet leave a long-lasting impression on the customer or client.

One very simple, but very common example of an organization not meeting expectations is when a customer calls and is told, *"I'll have someone get back to you on that within 48 hours"*—and the 48 hours comes and goes and you, the customer, still haven't been called back?

To one degree or another, brand trust has been compromised and the likelihood of the caller trusting any other messages that the company may convey through its marketing and advertising has been tarnished. And yet the company itself set the expectation that the phone call would be returned within 48 hours—the caller didn't.

I Often Cheat

That's right. As a consultant, when it comes to setting expectations, I often cheat.

If, for example, I'm asked how long it will take to submit a report, I often give the client a timeframe that is twice as long as I know it will take me to deliver, barring any unforeseen events.

By submitting the report in half the time the client expects to receive it, I've exceeded expectations. If some unforeseen event should arise, I've built in ample time to make my deadline and at the very least meet the expectation that I set.

Companies and organizations that fail to meet customer and client expectations—which most often they themselves set through their marketing and advertising—are at great risk of losing the trust of those very same customers and clients. And as we've already learned in *Aha! Moment #1*, a good brand is all about earning and maintaining trust.

"Let's give this some thought"

Questions to initiate and stimulate staff and board discussions

- How much are we relying on our marketing, advertising and public relations to convey our brand?

- If the answer is "a lot," are the messages we are conveying through those media true and supportable?

- At the very least, are the people responsible for our marketing, advertising and public relations aware of our brand and the messages we want to convey, or do they operate independently and in a silo-like environment, separate from other parts of the organization?

- When we set expectations, either large or small through our marketing and advertising—or simply over the phone—are we capable of meeting those expectations? If not, why not? And what changes do we need to make to ensure that every expectation, or promise, we make can be—and *is*—met?

Aha! Moment #3

Your Logo is <u>Not</u> Your Brand

> *"Truth is, logos don't really do much of anything . . . . They don't make you cooler. They don't make the product better. In fact a logo means nothing. Unless of course, the company behind it means something."*
>
> Hyundai auto ad

Your Logo is <u>Not</u> Your Brand

Your Logo is a Banner for Your Brand

In 2005, when I used the Internet as a research tool for my first book, *Branding for Success*, and typed "brand" or "branding" into the search field, I was led mostly to the websites of design firms. These companies promised to give their clients a good brand by creating an attractive logo for them, complete with a pleasing color scheme and perhaps a tagline thrown in, as well.

As a result of these kinds of promotions, many organizations continue to spend an inordinate amount of time, energy and money developing logos and taglines believing they are creating their brands, when in fact a logo and tagline are simply the banners for the brand. A brand drills much deeper into the core values of an organization.

> **Many organizations continue to spend an inordinate amount of time, energy and money developing logos and taglines believing they are creating their brands.**

It's What's Behind Your Logo that Matters

One of the most recognized and ubiquitous logos in the world is the McDonalds' golden arches. Yet, when you see that logo on billboards or perched atop a hundred-foot high pole on the side of the highway, all that logo is saying is, *"Here we are. McDonalds."* Nothing more; nothing less.

The golden arches logo is the banner—it carries the message—for the company brand that says we offer inexpensive food served quickly in a clean, safe, family-friendly environment. These are the brand characteristics, conveyed by the logo, that McDonalds customers have come to trust—and expect.

Now let's say—hypothetically—that one day you respond to the golden arches logo and stop at a McDonalds you haven't been to before and find that the menu is not the same, or the food tastes different, it's priced more expensively than what you've come to expect, and the place is something less than clean and doesn't seem particularly family friendly.

The McDonalds logo—those golden arches—that attracted you to the place is exactly the same as you remember it at other McDonalds establishments. But I would venture to say that your trust in the brand has probably diminished somewhat. And should this be a recurring experience I'd bet dollars to donuts you might stop "lovin' it" at McDonalds.

Aha!

No matter how attractive or recognizable your logo or how catchy your tagline, a brand is not a cosmetic that you apply to your organization to make it appealing. Rather, your brand is an honest and true reflection of who you are, what you do, how you do it and why anyone should care. In short, it's your DNA.

> **Your brand is an honest and true reflection of who you are, what you do, how you do it and why anyone should care. In short, it's your DNA.**

If all you have is a catchy logo and tagline without the commitment, willingness and ability to fulfill whatever promises they convey, then what you have is all sizzle—and it won't take long for your target audiences to see the smoke and mirrors and to realize there's no substance.

Whenever I bring up the McDonalds example in any of my workshops, I always get one or more people who adamantly say, *"I don't care how cheap, fast or family-friendly McDonalds is, I'm not going there."*

My response is, *"That's fine. But what has McDonalds' logo and brand accomplished?"*

Just because you have a logo that is hugely visible, highly recognizable and heavily advertised, and people, over time, have come to trust—and expect—what the brand represents doesn't necessarily equate to universal brand love.

What a well-branded product, company or organization does, however, is help people make an educated decision. *"Do I want to buy that company's product, or take advantage of that institution's services, or affiliate myself with that organization or political party?"*

If all you've been able to accomplish through your branding efforts is to project a true and accurate account of who you are, what you do, how you do it and why anyone should care, you've accomplished a lot—regardless of how well your logo is recognized.

"Let's give this some thought"

Questions to initiate and stimulate staff and board discussions

- Are we paying more attention to protecting our logo than we are to protecting our brand, meaning everything our logo is suppose to represent?

- Do our clients and customers even know what our logo looks like?

- If so, does our logo convey to them our brand? For example, just as McDonalds golden arches logo instantly conveys the message of inexpensive food served quickly in a clean, safe, family-friendly environment, does our logo convey who we are, what we do, how we do it and why anyone should care?

- If not, how can we better link our logo with our brand messages and vice versa?

Aha! Moment #4

Branding is Not the Sole Responsibility of Your
Communications, Marketing or
Public Relations Departments

"Quality is everyone's responsibility."

W. Edwards Deming
American scientist

Branding is Not the Sole Responsibility of Your Communications, Marketing or Public Relations Departments

Director of First Brand Impressions

> A good brand manager knows that his or her company's or organization's brand is in the hands of *EVERYONE* affiliated with the organization.

A good brand manager knows that his or her company's or organization's brand is in the hands of *EVERYONE* affiliated with the organization, from employees to board members to volunteers, as well as clients and customers. If it helps, consider the person who answers your phones your "Director of First Brand Impressions."

A True Story

I needed to change my flight plans and dreaded going through the process.

I'd done it with other airlines, and it was always a protracted, frustrating ordeal. To make matters worse, this particular morning I was on a deadline and had little time to spare.

I braced myself for dealing either with an automaton-like personality, or worse yet, the dreaded *"Press 1 for this . . . . Press 2 for that . . . . Press 3 . . . . Press 4 . . . . and if you'd like this menu repeated, please press . . . . "* Yikes! I drew a deep breath and made the call.

"Hello, my name is Susie. How may I help you today?"

I paused, dumbfounded!

"Are you a real person?" I replied, after propping up my jaw.

"Yes," she said in a friendly, receptive voice. *"My name is Susie. How may I help you?"*

"Well, Susie, my name is Larry, and I have a problem. I need to make a change to my departure time to New Orleans."

"That's no problem, Larry," she said. *"Just tell me what changes you need to make."*

I did, and in the process we laughed and joked about my initial anxiety about making the call. I was off the phone in less than 10 minutes—and didn't even mind paying the fee to make the change to my ticket.

> **I was off the phone in less than 10 minutes—and didn't even mind paying the fee to make the change to my ticket.**

But before hanging up I asked Susie for her supervisor's telephone number and called to compliment on how well Susie had served me over the phone. *"Susie's a great Director of First Brand Impressions,"* I told her supervisor, without reservation. *"And I'll fly with Southwest Airlines any chance I get."*

But What Really Happened?

After getting off the phone, I tried to analyze what had just happened. What had Susie done to make me want to spend the extra time to call her supervisor—on a morning when I was pressed for time, at that?

My answer was surprisingly simple: Susie was just doing her job, albeit in a consistently competent, friendly manner. Nothing more; nothing less.

Isn't it sad, I thought, how low our expectations have become for receiving good service—and how much we recognize and appreciate it when we *are* served well.

> **Isn't it sad, I thought, how low our expectations have become for receiving good service—and how much we recognize and appreciate it when we *are* served well.**

Aha!

The overwhelming majority of first personal contacts to most organizations, other than website hits, come over the phone. Yet we often overlook the critical impressions those contacts have on callers.

I don't know about you, but in my years of calling hundreds of organizations and dealing with countless "phone receptionists," I've often been given bad information, talked to as if I were an imposition rather than a valued customer, put on interminable hold, made to feel like I had just woken the person up, or been treated downright rudely. Sometimes I don't even get past the receptionist and I'm already questioning whether or not I want to do business with this group.

> **Sometimes I don't even get past the receptionist and I'm already questioning whether or not I want to do business with this group.**

Take the test. Call your own organization, and then ask yourself, *"Was I received in a way that would make me want to call this organization again?"*

What does it take to turn a "receptionist" into an effective "Director of First Brand Impressions"?

- **Put the right personality in the job.** Hire someone who is competent, capable, outgoing and truly enjoys interacting with people.

- **Educate them.** Through appropriate training, let them know what's expected of them when they answer your phones, and what it means to "live" the brand when it comes to being knowledgeable, respectful and pleasant to others.

- **Value that person(s).** So often, the people who answer our phones are at the bottom of the organizational chart. They're often paid the least, get invited to the fewest meetings, and receive little attention, recognition or respect from others on staff. Yet, when it comes to first brand impressions, they are where the rubber hits the road. Give them the respect they deserve, and the results may surprise you.

- **Make them "heroes."** Let them know the critical role they play in helping your organization sell its products and services or achieve its mission. This goes for all "support staff." If an important document needs to go out at 5 p.m. on a Friday and there's no toner or paper in the copy machine, I'll guarantee you that neither your board chair nor your executive director is the most important person in your organization at that moment.

And, if you must use an answering machine, please, please make it sound like a human being recorded the message. And keep the menu options to a minimum. I beg you!

I've had people say, *"I work in finance. What does that have to do with branding?"*

My response: *"Just ask the folks who worked for Enron, Arthur Anderson, Fannie Mae, Freddie Mac, Bear Stearns, Lehman Brothers, AIG and countless others how much their finance folks had to do with their organizations' brands—and their livelihoods!"*

All of which underscores how each and every employee is responsible for protecting the brand.

"Let's give this some thought"

Questions to initiate and stimulate staff and board discussions

- Are we under the impression that our brand is solely the domain of our marketing, advertising and public relations folks?

- Does everyone in our organization—from support staff to board members—know what our brand is and what's expected of them with respect to "living" our brand?

- Do we have the right people in the right positions?

- If so, have we educated them to let them know what's expected of them?

- Regardless of where people are on our organizational chart, have we made them feel truly valued and respected?

- Have we informed them of the critical role they play in helping us achieve our objectives?

- Maybe the next time we need someone to answer our phones or staff our front desk we might want to advertise for a "Director of First Brand Impression" rather than for a "Receptionist."

Aha! Moment #5

Nothing Escapes the Public's Eyes

> *"Consumers build an image [of a brand] as birds build nests. From the scraps and straws they chance upon."*
>
> Jeremy Bullmore
> Marketing Guru

Nothing Escapes the Public's Eye

Pay Attention to Details

I was just about to make a positive remark about the attractive design on the cover of a document, when a colleague of the person whose department was responsible for putting the piece together blurted out, *"Hey, Jim, the county's name is spelled wrong on the cover of your report."*

You could have heard a pin drop as Jim (not his real name) flinched with embarrassment.

This scene unfolded during one of my branding workshops to a group of 20 county government leaders. It was at the point in my presentation when I gathered everyone around a large conference table to peer-review each other's printed materials. The purpose: To determine how well the materials reflected their respective department's brands.

Was the error that was pointed out on the cover of the document a mere typo? Hardly. The document in question happened to be a financial report scheduled to be released to the public.

Aha!

I saw a teachable moment.

Reassuring Jim that I was not trying to embarrass anyone, but rather attempting to make a point, I asked the group, *"If the county's name is misspelled on the cover of this document how can we be guaranteed that the page after page of dollar figures inside are correct?"*

> **"If the county's name is misspelled on the cover of this document how can we be guaranteed that the page after page of dollar figures inside are correct?"**

In effect, the typo was a breach in the brand trust Jim's department was trying so hard to restore under new leadership.

The episode reaffirmed what I had been telling the group from the outset: that there is nothing an organization can say or do that isn't a reflection on its brand, everything from how courteously its phones are answered, to whether or not staff is dressed appropriately and, yes, even typos—especially if you're responsible for financial data or customers' names.

> **There is nothing an organization can say or do that isn't a reflection on its brand.**

What the Public Perceives

The fact is, the public picks up on all kinds of cues that provide them with insights—be they right or wrong—about who you are, what you do, how you do it and why they should care, which I believe are the key questions any good brand must address.

Here's an example that demonstrates the other side of this coin.

Many of the local affiliates of a former national client of mine operate thrift shops, which represent a significant portion of their annual local revenue streams. I had the good fortune to be asked to tour several of these facilities located in different parts of the country and to give my impression of what I saw.

In short, I was truly astounded on how neat, orderly and well organized all of the thrift shops were kept.

Things weren't piled on the floor, as one might expect in a thrift shop, and shoppers were not forced to rummage through boxes to find what they were looking for.

Rather, floor space was divided into attractive departments, some using iconic art work to let customers know which department they were in; the clothes were all neatly folded or hung on racks, some attractively placed on mannequins; the used furniture and electronic equipment had all been repaired or restored and laid out as it might be in a high-end department store; the jewelry was all sorted and neatly displayed.

In short, the message these shops implicitly conveyed to me was, *"If this organization is such a good steward of donated used clothing and furniture it must be paying the same kind of attention to detail with respect to the funds these thrift shops bring in and the services the organization provides to its clients. This may be an organization I'd like to support."*

Rightly or wrongly, perception is reality.

Rightly or wrongly, perception is reality. And the perception this organization was tacitly but convincingly conveying was *"Trust us. We know what we're doing."* That's a powerful and desirable brand message any organization would be happy to own, and speaks to the importance of paying attention to details when it comes to the public's perceptions regarding you and your brand.

"Let's give this some thought"

Questions to initiate and stimulate staff and board discussions

- Do we diligently pay attention to details across all of our lines of business and in everything we communicate?

- For example, before we distribute press releases, reports and other printed materials are they edited for typos and accuracy?

- Do we have systems in place to prevent inaccuracies?

- Do we hold people accountable if they fail to pay attention to details?

Aha! Moment #6

Everyone in Your Organization Needs to be
Singing from the Same Song Sheet

"Word of mouth is the best medium of all."

William Bernbach
Creative Director

Everyone in Your Organization Needs to be Singing from the Same Song Sheet

Reduce the Noise

It doesn't matter how good the choir is. If everyone is singing from different song sheets—it's just noise!

The same holds true for an organization's brand. If everyone is sending out different messages about what the brand represents, it confuses the audiences you are trying to reach and influence.

> **If everyone is sending out different messages about what the brand represents, it confuses the audiences you are trying to reach and influence.**

One of the best ways to keep everyone on message is to create what I call a "messaging package."

A messaging package is simply a compilation of the core messages you want your brand to convey. Its purpose is to help you and your staff stay on message whenever you communicate information about your organization, whether it's in a press release, speech, marketing materials, casual conversations or any other communication opportunities.

A good messaging package is the touchstone for your brand and answers the questions: Who are we? What do we do? How do we do it? And why should anyone care enough to support us?

Your messaging package should include the following:

Tagline

A tagline is a catchy, quick-identifying reference, usually no more than five to seven words. A good tagline will trigger the imagination, interest and emotions of your target audiences. Think of Nike's *"Just do it!"* or the American Red Cross's *"Together, we can save a life."*

Your tagline should be incorporated into all your materials, including signage, stationery, banners, media materials, website, etc.

Positioning statement

A positioning statement is often referred to as an "elevator speech," something that can be stated quickly—within 20 seconds or so—to someone who knows little, if anything, about your organization. It is perhaps the most important component of your messaging package and should be compelling and to the point.

For example, I'm attending a conference and while in the hotel elevator someone notices my nametag, which also includes the name of my business:

"I see that your company is listed in the conference brochure. What exactly is it that you do?"

My immediate reply is:

"Checco Communications is a consulting firm that specializes in branding. I help organizations better define who they are, what they do, how they do it and why anyone should care."

It's short—I can usually get it out in 10 to 15 seconds—conversational in tone, and often sparks an interest in the listener. *"You know, my organization is having trouble explaining who we are and what we do. May I have one of your business cards?"*

Notice that in my brief elevator speech I do not include the fact that I've written books on branding or that I teach workshops or do motivational speaking on the subject. That's because the purpose of a positioning statement is not to educate people about every program, service or product your organization offers.

> **The purpose of a positioning statement is not to educate people about every program, service or product your organization offers.**

> **Rather your elevator speech should be designed to interest the listener in your overall mission.**

Rather your elevator speech should be designed to interest the listener in your overall mission, to get them to care enough about what you do—and your importance or added value to the community and customers you serve—so that they will want to learn more.

Which leads us to supporting statements . . . .

Supporting statements

Think of supporting statements as talking points that support your positioning statement. Supporting statements can be included into your speeches, presentations, printed materials, website and elsewhere.

You can create three supporting statements; you can create dozens of supporting statements that can be selectively used to target different audiences, such as customers, funders, the media, donors and others.

Supporting statements may address:

- Your core values (i.e. caring and responsive to the needs of customers; reliable, trustworthy business partner; good stewards of public/private funding, etc.)
- The range of products, programs and services you offer
- The impact of your work on the customers and people you serve, as well as the community, in general
- How long your organization has been in existence.

In short, supporting statements are just that—they bolster the brand by providing additional facts about your organization to various targeted audiences.

> **Supporting statements bolster the brand by providing additional facts about your organization to various targeted audiences.**

Logo

Your logo is the design cornerstone that should give all of your materials a consistent look, style and feel so that people can identify immediately with your organization. (Think of the Olympics and its five easily recognizable rings, Nike's swoosh, and the Red Cross's, well, red cross.)

In addition to being attractive and representative of your brand, think about the various ways you may use your logo and how difficult or expensive it may be to reproduce. Consider proportions as well. A detailed logo that looks great on a large banner may not reproduce well when it is reduced to fit on a business card. Also, how will it look in color, black and white, faxed, enlarged or reduced?

> **Your logo should be used uniformly and consistently on all your materials.**

Your logo should be used uniformly and consistently on all your materials, including annual reports, brochures, flyers, report covers, press releases, video covers, and so forth.

Creating an effective messaging package will take some time, energy and resources. But if used consistently, it's a great way to get everyone singing from the same song sheet, a way to produce harmony instead of noise when it comes to explaining who you are, what you do, how you do it—and why anyone should care enough to support you or buy your products.

Do the Research!

It's amazing how even well-crafted messages can be misunderstood.

As a child, did you ever play "Telephone"? It's a parlor game whereby players line up within whispering distance of each other. The player at the beginning of the line thinks of a phrase, and whispers it as quietly as possible to his or her neighbor. The neighbor then passes on the message to the next player to the best of his or her ability. The passing on of the message continues in this fashion until it reaches the player at the end of the line, who calls out the message he or she received.

More often than not the final message has little resemblance to the original phrase that started the game. This is typical of what happens in real life conversations, as well.

> **The best way to communicate to your target audiences is to craft messages that are clear, consistent, concise—and true!**

That's why the best way to communicate to your target audiences is to craft messages that are clear, consistent, concise—and true! This will take a bit of research (see Step 1 thru Step 5 below), but if done properly, the results are well worth the effort.

Step 1
Come to internal consensus about what you want to convey about your organization through your messaging. These messages may include the core values of your organizational culture, the kinds of products, programs or services you provide, how you provide them and so forth.

The best way to come to consensus around these messages is to conduct an internal SWOT (Strengths, Weaknesses, Opportunities and Threats) analysis. The goal of this introspective analysis—which gets its best results when key stakeholders are interviewed confidentially by a knowledgeable, objective third party—often goes beyond messaging and allows an organization, perhaps for the first time, to consciously identify and confidently promote its strengths, address its weaknesses, leverage its opportunities and prepare for the range of threats its stakeholders collectively may perceive.

Keep in mind that whatever messages come out of this process need to reflect your organization's story, not its fairytale. For example, if one of the strengths you identify is that your organization is a good steward of public funding, make sure that the attention, policies and procedures are in place to assure that that's the case, and stays the case—without exception!

Step 2
Conduct external research. Through focus groups, surveys or informal conversations, learn what your target audiences want to know about your company and its products and services. Are their current perceptions accurate about who you are and what you do? If not, why not, and how do you need to alter your messages to gain their attention, recognition and understanding?

> **Learn what your target audiences want to know about your company and its products and services.**

Step 3
Draft your messages. Use what you have learned through your internal SWOT analysis and external research to draft a messaging package that contains all the messages you believe are not only true and accurate about your organization, but also will resonate with your target audiences.

Step 4
Test your messages! Before going public with your messages, be sure to test them. (see *Aha! Moment # 7*).

Step 5

Teach and practice your messages. The goal of every organization and company should be *"to stay on message."* Therefore, make sure everyone affiliated with your organization knows the messages you seek to convey. The reason for this is that if everyone affiliated with your organization is sending out different messages, they tend to confuse your audiences. To truly understand who you are and what you do—and why they should support what you do!—your

> **Make sure everyone affiliated with your organization knows the messages you seek to convey.**

audiences need to receive clear, consistent and concise messages. A messaging package can help you do this. It can also take a lot of the anxiety out of talking about your organization, as well.

> **If *you* don't control your brand through clear, consistent and concise messaging, others will.**

The fact is that if *you* don't control your brand through clear, consistent and concise messaging, others will. And more often than not it will have the same results, as often happens when playing "Telephone."

"Let's give this some thought"

Questions to initiate and stimulate staff and board discussions

- Does everyone affiliated with our organization—including support staff and board members—know what to say about our organization when they're asked about who we are and what we do, or are we always shooting from the hip with our responses?

- Have we created a "messaging package" that includes a tagline, positioning statement ("elevator speech"), supporting statements and logo?

- If so, is everyone in our organization familiar with all the elements of the package and able to articulate our messages clearly and accurately?

- What are we doing to motivate those affiliated with our organization to use the messages in this package when they talk about us to others?

Aha! Moment #7
Test Your Messages

> *"Advertising people who ignore research are as dangerous as generals who ignore decodes of enemy signals."*
>
> David Ogilvy
> Advertising Executive

Test Your Messages

Different Words for Different Folks

I was part of a team conducting a focus group for a large national nonprofit client. The focus group comprised representatives from the financial sector, a target audience this particular organization was most interested in cultivating through its messaging.

One or more of the messages we were about to test had the words *"partners"* and *"partnership"* in them, which we thought were no-brainers. After all, they are simple, easy-to-understand words that convey affiliation, cooperation, collaboration, alliance, all the good stuff, right?

Wrong!

As the messages came up for the group's reaction, two bankers immediately raised their hands.

> **"In our industry, the words 'partners' and 'partnership' are loaded with legal implications,"** said one banker.

"In our industry, the words 'partners' and 'partnership' are loaded with legal implications," said one banker. *"We don't mind being recognized as 'working together' with this particular organization, but we'd rather not be identified as 'partners,'"* said the other.

Aha!

Had we allowed our client to go public with the original messages, chances are the impact that they might have had on their intended audience, namely potential financial sector funders, would have been the opposite from that which the organization was hoping for.

The lesson learned: It's not about how your messages are *delivered* but rather how they are *received* that makes all the difference.

> **It's not about how your messages are *delivered* but rather how they are *received* that makes all the difference.**

Most organizations aren't aware of that lesson, so they shoot from the hip when it comes to talking about themselves. They don't pay enough attention to the messages they send out and often have no idea how those messages are resonating with the very audiences they are seeking to positively influence.

So, do the research. Conduct small focus group tests or survey your target audiences to determine if the messages you have created resonate with them. If they don't, conduct more research to learn what messages *will* influence them in a way that honestly reflects your company or organization.

"Let's give this some thought"

Questions to initiate and stimulate staff and board discussions

- How sensitive and aware are we regarding how our messages are received by our target audiences?

- Do we speak industry jargon that they don't understand?

- How much do we know about those audiences, and what they want or need to hear from us?

- If we believe we have created clear, concise and consistent messages, have we gone the extra step and done the research to know whether or not the precise language we use in those messages actually resonates with the audiences we are striving to reach?

Aha! Moment #8

If You're the Leader, Focus on Others

"The leader has to be practical and a realist, yet must talk the language of the visionary and the idealist."

Eric Hoffer
Author, Philosopher

If You're the Leader, Focus on Others

Two Schools of Thought

No brand can ultimately succeed in the absence of good management leadership.

No brand, no matter how good the products, services or messaging it represents, can ultimately succeed in the absence of good management leadership.

What does it mean to be a good leader?

Two primary schools of thought seem to prevail: One is that leaders are born, not made; that they are anointed from on high or somehow are genetically programmed to go to the head of the line to lead the rest of us.

Those who find themselves in leadership positions must manifest certain leadership traits if they hope to be successful.

The other school of thought says that through instruction and mentoring, leadership skills can be taught, if not to all, at least to many people.

The bottom line is that those who find themselves in leadership positions, regardless of whether or not leadership was bestowed upon them as a natural birthright or they came upon it as an acquired skill—or simply by accident—must manifest certain leadership traits if they hope to be successful.

In my experience, good leadership is as much, if not more, about charting a course for others as it is for leaders charting a course for their organizations or for themselves.

The Hero's Journey

In his book, *The Hero with a Thousand Faces*, the late Joseph Campbell, a distinguished professor and author of several books on mythology, laid out what he believed to be the story, or journey, of the hero. It is a story so intrinsic to and so deeply seated in our human psyche that it predates early Greek mythology, and comes full circle to be featured in today's popular culture. It is a story that is timeless and told repeatedly.

In his book, Campbell goes into great detail regarding the hero's journey. The abridged version of his theory goes something like this: A hero is created when an ordinary person is taken from their normal surroundings, survives extraordinary hardships with the help of a mentor, learns profound life lessons and returns to his place of origin where, as a role model and hero, he or she passes these lessons on to others. *"The hero's task,"* wrote Campbell, *"always has been and always will be to bring new life to a dying culture."*

> **"The hero's task always has been and always will be to bring new life to a dying culture."**

Think of motion pictures such as *Star Wars, Rocky, The Wizard of Oz, It's a Wonderful Life* as archetypical examples of fictional hero's journeys that have made their way into our cultural subconscious. If you need real-life heroes, think of Abraham Lincoln, Ghandi or Nelson Mandela, and their journeys to redefine and bring new life and ideas to their countries.

Because the model Campbell outlined for this journey is so sensible and appealing, all kinds of leadership forums, self-help groups and others have adopted and adapted his model to meet their respective needs.

A Twist on Campbell's Model

No doubt Campbell's model of the hero's journey easily lends itself to leadership training. But as I said before, I also believe that the indicator of a leader's true leadership ability may depend not only on whether or not he or she can map out and survive a hero's journey for himself or herself, but whether or not these same people can successfully map out a hero's journey for those they seek to lead, as well.

To my way of thinking, to be good leaders, executives, managers, teachers, coaches and others need to use their instincts, sensibilities, intellect and reason to look outside of themselves. They intrinsically should understand that inside each and every one of those they are charged to lead is a hero aching to be born, regardless of his or her position in life or where they stand on the organizational chart. The fact is that as individuals, we are all eager to be recognized, be it socially, intellectually or professionally.

> **As individuals, we are all eager to be recognized, be it socially, intellectually or professionally.**

Therefore, what is required of a good leader is an inherent respect for others. In addition, he or she needs to set achievable goals, as well as be able to listen, and provide positive feedback and mentoring so as to be able to launch others on successful hero journeys.

> **What is required of a good leader is an inherent respect for others.**

An Early Lesson in Leadership

As a young man, I worked my way around the world and took on a number of odd and interesting jobs. What follows is a true personal story. It's an experience—and lesson—that for whatever reasons, has stuck with me for decades.

<u>He stated our goal</u>
"It needs to be unloaded by the end of the day!"

We all looked at each other, seven yard hands working for a Western Australia transport company. The assignment was to unload what seemed like an endless boxcar filled with 40-pound sacks of flour. I overheard one of my co-workers mumble, *"He must be joking!"*

It was one of those dog days of summer, with the temperature and humidity both in the high 90s. We all knew that inside the 50-foot long metal boxcar the temperature would be well over 120 miserable, sweaty degrees. No one even dared to venture a guess on how many sacks of flour the boxcar contained.

"All right, gentlemen, we're going to do this in bucket-brigade fashion," said, Mac, our new gang boss, a ruddy-faced, barrel-chested Scot who none of us knew very well.

<u>He stood beside us</u>
As we grumbled and slowly lined up to form our bucket brigade, Mac did an astonishing thing for a yard boss. Instead of assigning himself to some sanitized, rah-rah leadership role in the shade, he took off his shirt, climbed into the super-heated boxcar and started passing sacks of flour to the next man in line. He never belittled any of us for our initial grumbling. He recognized that what we were *all* about to do was going to be hard work.

<u>He took care of us</u>
Over the next several hours Mac rotated us so that no one was ever in the super-heated boxcar for more than 15 or 20 minutes. Mac also made sure we took several breaks and drank plenty of water so we wouldn't get dehydrated, which conveyed to us the message that he was looking after our best interests.

There was no coaxing, cajoling or bullying on Mac's part; he simply set an expectation, defined our goal clearly right from the start, and worked alongside us the entire time to get the job done.

There was no coaxing, cajoling or bullying on Mac's part.

He made it fun

In fact, Mac's energy, quick wit and humor made us all laugh and joke. We even broke into song—despite the fact that flour seeping from some of the burlap sacks and mixing with the perspiration on our shirtless bodies was turning us into white, ghoulish-looking creatures. But we simply considered it part of the job. In fact, our pasty appearance served to bond us together, identified us as a unit—especially during breaks, when we mingled with those who were not assigned to our gang.

He made us a team

Intentionally or not, Mac had effectively transported us psychologically from what we considered our daily routine task of mindless lifting and toting—all part of an ordinary day's work for a minimum-wage yard hand—to something that resembled a meaningful endeavor.

Soon we were no longer passing sacks of flour to each other—but tossing them. We were no longer a pack of disgruntled workers, but rather a team working together on a mission, toward a goal.

> **We were no longer a pack of disgruntled workers, but rather a team working together on a mission, toward a goal.**

He rewarded us

We unloaded that boxcar in record time.

After we had accomplished our goal, Mac thanked us and bought us soft drinks to quench our thirst as each of us sat around sharing stories of the day and laughing.

I doubt any of our fellow yard hands worked as hard as we did that day, certainly none looked as ghastly—and I dare say, none felt as engaged or had the same sense of ownership in their work as we did.

Aha!

Regardless of whether he did it consciously or not, Mac had successfully mapped out a hero's journey for us.

> **Consciously or not, Mac had successfully mapped out a hero's journey for us.**

Despite what others might think of as low-paying menial labor, I went to sleep that night with a profound sense of satisfaction and accomplishment—and with a lesson in leadership that I remember to this day, more than 30 years later.

The fact is that no one exists in a vacuum. We are acted upon by—and react to—the environments in which we live, play and work. These environments may either be conducive to our living, playing and working our best—or not.

> No one exists in a vacuum. We are acted upon by—and react to—the environments in which we live, play and work.

It follows therefore that one of the responsibilities of a good leader is to ensure that the people he or she leads are responding to the best possible environments that they, as leaders, can create.

Further Thoughts on Leadership

Put organizational goals in perspective
Hyper-focusing on organizational goals most often results in that old fallback position that the end justifies the means. This leadership model almost always leads to a management structure and corporate culture that erroneously perceives workers as dispensable tools for achieving business objectives. Instead, they should be perceived as the indispensable employees they truly are for helping achieve overall organizational success.

Leadership is a contact sport
Good leaders don't hole themselves up in ivory towers. Neither do they lead by being in front of their people. Good leaders lead by working beside their people, letting them know the valuable role each plays in achieving the company's mission. and that *"we're all working together as a team to achieve our common goals."*

> Good leaders lead by working beside their people, letting them know the valuable role each plays in achieving the company's mission.

Don't confuse charisma with leadership
There are many charismatic personalities who have an innate ability to draw people to them but have nowhere to lead them. Don't be fooled by a pretty face or glib talk. Instead, ask *"Where is this person capable of taking us? How do they propose getting us there? And is that place the right destination for our organization?"*

Don't confuse power with leadership
Just because you can tell people what to do doesn't mean you're leading them. It could mean that they are doing what you tell them to do out of fear of reprisal, which is a push-pull mechanism that may work in the short term, but over the long haul it inevitably leads to a dispirited, lifeless and often disgruntled workforce.

"Thank you" is often the most undervalued
expression in the English language
Many leaders view kindness as a weakness, even in themselves, and that thanking others for what they have done is somehow beneath them.

On the contrary, *"thank you"* is an essential expression of gratitude when it comes to acknowledging someone for what they've done. It bespeaks respect for the person, as well as the value you place on what they've accomplished. A sincere, heartfelt "Thank you" is a small investment that can return huge dividends for those who lead—as well as for those who are being led.

> *"Thank you"* is an essential expression of gratitude when it comes to acknowledging someone for what they've done.

"Let's give this some thought"

Questions to initiate and stimulate staff and board discussions

- Do our organization's leaders and managers understand that they must look beyond themselves and be able to create hero's journeys for those they seek to lead?

- Does our company's overall leadership style lead to the creation of a healthy work environment for staff at all levels of the organizational chart?

- What is the current state of our employees' morale? If it's low, might that be a function of poor leadership?

- Do we have the right people in leadership positions?

- If not, are we prepared to make the necessary hard decisions to get the right people in those positions?

- What's at stake if we don't?

Aha! Moment #9

When Leadership Fails

"The key to successful leadership is influence, not authority."

Kenneth Blanchard

Aha! Moment #9

When Leadership Fails

Poor Leadership Often Creates Toxic Work Environments

We've all sat in on those meetings—you know, the ones around the conference table when a decision is about to be made. Knowing something of consequence is going to be discussed and decided on, the first thing most of us do is start to take a reading of the others gathered around the table with us. We note their general moods, attitudes, facial expressions, side conversations, even their body language.

> **"Which way is the crowd leaning and how much of a risk am I willing to take if I decide to go against the will of the majority?"**

"Which way is the crowd leaning and how much of a risk am I willing to take if I decide to go against the will of the majority?" is something we often consciously or unconsciously ask ourselves.

It's a difficult position to be in, especially when personal standing with one's boss and co-workers is on the line, perhaps even one's job.

A Case in Point

On Tuesday, October 26, 2007, the United States Federal Emergency Management Agency, better known as FEMA, held a press conference—of sorts. Wild fires were burning out of control in Southern California. At least 1,500 homes had been destroyed and over 500,000 acres of land burned from Santa Barbara County to the U.S. Mexican border. Nine people died as a direct result of the fires; 85 others were injured, including at least 61 firefighters. Tragic, newsworthy events.

Evidently FEMA was desperate to get information out to the public about the assistance it was providing, as well as to "spin" what the agency believed was the good work it was doing to help victims.

Reporters were notified a mere 15 minutes before the start of the event. It should not have surprised anyone at FEMA that none were able to attend this quickly assembled "news" event.

The briefing itself had all the markings of a legitimate press conference. FEMA's press secretary at one point cautioned that he would allow just *"two more questions,"* then called later for a *"last question."* In appearance it all seemed authentic enough.

The problem was that in the absence of any legitimate press, those who were posing the questions were FEMA employees—including the agency's deputy director of public affairs, as well as its director of external affairs! They planted themselves in the audience to query their own agency's Deputy Administrator with questions *The New York Times* would later call *"decidedly friendly,"* such as *"What type of commodities are you pledging to California?"* *"What lessons learned from Katrina have been applied?"* and *"Are you happy with FEMA's response so far?"*

Then-Homeland Security Chief, Michael Chertoff said it was the *"stupidest"* thing he'd ever seen in government.

Of course, to the great embarrassment of FEMA and the administration, this was all quickly unearthed and endlessly reported by the media, in particular *The Washington Post.* In the end, FEMA was forced to issue an apology, calling it *"an error in judgment."* Then-Homeland

Security Chief, Michael Chertoff, put it more bluntly when he said it was the *"stupidest"* thing he'd ever seen in government.

But the question remains: How did this public agency, whose reputation, or brand, was already in tatters because of its dismal response in the wake of Hurricane Katrina just two years earlier, expect to get away with this ruse? After all, this happened in Washington, DC, the center of government and the world's biggest fishbowl, filled with predatory media outlets constantly on the prowl for just such bureaucratic snafus.

Where was the rational, commonsense braveheart sitting at the conference table while this plan was being hatched who should have been frantically waving his or her arms and shouting, *"This is not the right thing for us to be doing. Our agency is already suffering from the public's lack of trust in our ability to carry out our mission. If and when this gets discovered* (and how could it not!)*, it's not going to help our reputation. It's only going to reinforce the public's distrust and perception of our ineptitude."*

"This is not the right thing for us to be doing."

Aha!

The Cascade Effect

What most likely happened at FEMA during that fateful meeting might be described as the result of groupthink, or "information cascade."

The problem often starts when people make their decisions in sequence rather than all at once. In his book entitled *"The Wisdom of Crowds,"* author James Surowiecki says that *"The fundamental problem with an information cascade is that after a certain point it becomes rational for people to stop paying attention to their own information—their private information—and to start looking instead at the actions of others and imitate them."*

I would add that this type of negative cascade effect is exacerbated in organizations where senior and mid-level managers would rather be seen as authoritative figures, obeyed and followed, than transformative leaders who, when presented with constructive criticism, take it into serious consideration and possibly alter their mindsets.

An information cascade is similar to groupthink, whereby a group of people manifest conformity in their thoughts and behavior, especially an unthinking acceptance of majority opinions.

Groupthink reinforces collective thought, not so much from a base of common sense, or rational thinking, but because of a strong hierarchical pecking order often in combination with peer pressure, which often results in the inability to speak truth to authority.

> **An information cascade is similar to groupthink, whereby a group of people manifest conformity in their thoughts and behavior.**

The Inability to Speak Truth to Authority

A 2008 survey by the Ethics Resource Center found that nearly 60 percent of all government workers reported witnessing violations of ethical standards, policy or laws in their workplace within the previous year. Fifty-eight percent who saw misconduct did not report it because they did not believe managers would take action; 30 percent feared they would face retaliation if they reported what they saw.

In short, these government workers were forced to execute their work responsibilities in environments where the ability to speak truth to authority was either stifled or nonexistent.

The kinds of misconduct most frequently observed, according to the survey were: abusive behavior (23%); safety violations (21%); lying to employees (20%); putting one's own interests ahead of the organization's (20%).

> **When trust and the ability to speak one's truth to authority are leached from the environment, many organizations either fail in their missions or create emotionally unhealthy workplaces.**

Other studies show that the private and nonprofit sectors don't fare much better.

The simple fact is that when trust and the ability to speak one's truth to authority are leached from the environment, many organizations either fail in their missions or create emotionally unhealthy workplaces, which result in bad decision making. In toxic environments like these, it doesn't take long to reach a tipping point where negative groupthink and the information cascade replace common sense.

What Can be Done.

This is an organizational cultural issue that starts with leadership style. What can be done to ameliorate a toxic work environment?

- **Allow staff to speak its truth to your authority without fear of reprisal or retribution**. Often the best way to have this happen is to tell staff that they will not suffer from being frank, both with you and each other, about problems they see, but that disagreements should be expressed politely, without heat, with evidence, and preferably in private rather than public.

- **Avoid bully management**. This style of management may work to meet short-term tactical deadlines but damages morale, and thus has a negative effect not only on achieving long-term strategic goals, but also on the staff's ability and willingness to think in more daring, creative ways.

- **Solicit the opinions of others**. Employees, even if their demands are not met, at least want to know that they've been listened to and that what they say will be given serious consideration. Listening can often diffuse tense workplace situations and environments.

- **Be open to change.** Ideological thinking may not be the best strategy, especially in fast-changing times. Be open to, rather than threatened by new ideas that come from employees.

- **Be respectful of staff.** Again, as stated previously in this book, *"Thank you"* are the two most undervalued words in the English language. Coupled with *"Good morning"* and a smile every now and then, saying *"Thank you"* can often relieve a lot of daily office tension—and produce better, and more honest, decision making—and consequently, better brands.

"Let's give this some thought"

Questions to initiate and stimulate staff and board discussions

- Have we created a workplace environment that allows employees to speak truth to authority without reprisal?

- If not, what changes do we need to make to enable employee information and feelings to flow more freely and without fear of retribution?

- In our meetings, who sets the tone, and is that tone conducive to open, honest discussions, or are those in charge of our meetings simply looking for their thoughts and ideas to be rubber stamped? In other words, do we fall prey to the cascade effect and groupthink?

- Are we truly conscious of the fact that stifling open and honest dialogue between our employees and management also stifles our ability to be as daring, risk-taking and creative as we might be?

Aha! Moment #10

A Disgruntled Workforce Can be a Branding Nightmare

> *"It isn't what they say about you, it's what they whisper."*
>
> Errol Flynn
> Actor

A Disgruntled Workforce Can be a Branding Nightmare

Value Your Assets

I had just finished conducting a focus group for a large national nonprofit organization. Of the 20 focus group participants, all had left the room but one, a woman who lingered at the back of the room, seemingly waiting for all the others to leave.

When the door to the room finally closed, she walked up to me and said, *"Larry, thank you. I've been working for this organization for 14 years, and this is the first time anyone has asked my opinion about anything."*

I knew that the organization's executive director for whom I had just conducted the focus group had been on the job for less than 18 months and within another year or so would move on. Yet here was this woman who I realized during the focus group session harbored a lot of institutional memory and was willing

> **Here was this woman who harbored a lot of institutional memory—yet in all of her 14 years of employment at this organization, no one had asked her opinion of anything!**

to speak up—*yet in all of her 14 years of employment at this organization, no one had asked her opinion of anything!*

Aha!

Not only was this organization not leveraging a valuable employee asset, it had not succeeded in creating a workplace environment in which all employees felt valued, respected and recognized for their work. What kind of a brand image do you suppose this woman was promoting about the organization any time someone asked her about her job or where she worked?

Fact is, a disgruntled worker—worse yet, a disgruntled workforce—can turn into a branding nightmare, because while you, as a leader, are doing everything possible to raise the visibility and to create a strong and positive brand reputation for your company or organization, your employees are giving anyone who is willing to listen an earful about their negative impression of their work environment.

People move on to other jobs for a whole variety of reasons. How are they going to talk about you as a past employer?

"Let's give this some thought"

Questions to initiate and stimulate staff and board discussions

- Do we value all of our employees?

- If so, how do we demonstrate that value in meaningful, ongoing ways?

- If not, how can we better value and respect all of our employees?

- Once again, we need to ask ourselves what kind of workplace environment do we need to create that will allow our employees to speak well of us to the pubic and, in essence, become truly good brand ambassadors for our organization.

Aha! Moment #11

Even the Best Thinkers Can
Lose Track of Their Goals

"Creativity involves breaking out of established patterns in order to look at things in a different way."

Edward De Bono
Physician, Author, Inventor

Even the Best Thinkers Can Lose Track of Their Goals

Don't be Complacent

On October 23, 2008, Alan Greenspan, former chairman of the Federal Reserve, testified before members of the U.S. House of Representatives Oversight and Government Reform Committee. The economy was in a shambles. The U.S. Treasury, under Secretary Henry Paulson, was in the midst of planning a $700 billion bailout to help stop the bleeding; our national economic woes were having a devastating impact on world markets; and Congress was searching for answers.

The hearing was contentious. After much verbal jousting with Committee members, Mr. Greenspan conceded that his worldview of how markets work—a view he admitted he had held for more than 40 years—was wrong, and that he was *"shocked"* by this personal revelation. He remarked in his own inimitable way that he *"made a mistake in presuming that the self-interests of organizations, specifically banks and others, were such as that they*

> **For the past 40 years Mr. Greenspan had always been convinced that the *"invisible hand"* of the marketplace would cure its own ills.**

were best capable of protecting their own shareholders and their equity in their firms."

In other words, for the past 40 years Mr. Greenspan had always been convinced that the *"invisible hand"* of the marketplace would cure its own ills.

At the very least, his recollection of the savings and loan scandal of the 1980s and the more recent dot.com bubble of 2000-01 should have raised some red flags in his thinking. Yet, after all his years at the helm of the Federal Reserve, Mr. Greenspan stuck by his beliefs and always advocated for minimal rather than more regulation of the invisible hand of the marketplace.

In an effort to explain how the economy had gotten to a point of near collapse, Mr. Greenspan went on to testify in the hearing that the Federal Reserve was *"as good an economic organization as exists. If all those extraordinarily capable people were unable to foresee the development of this critical problem . . . we have to ask ourselves: Why is that?"* He answered his own question by saying *". . . that we're not smart enough as people. We just cannot see events that far in advance."*

Was the Federal Reserve truly not *"smart enough"* or was it simply unable to break from its traditional thought patterns?

Perhaps Mr. Greenspan's phalanx of Federal Reserve economists, armed with some of the most sophisticated computer modeling ever known, truly could not foresee what the future might bring. However, signs pointing to the way things were heading were seemingly everywhere—if one were looking for them, that is.

> **Signs pointing to the way things were heading were seemingly everywhere—if one were looking for them, that is.**

Heads in the Sand Rather than Ears to the Ground

In an in-depth article in the December 2008 edition of *Vanity Fair* magazine writer Niall Ferguson used Detroit, Michigan, as a case in point to help explain the housing debacle. *"For several years agents and brokers selling subprime mortgages had been flooding Detroit with radio, television, and direct-mail advertisements, offering what sounded like attractive deals,"* Ferguson wrote. He went on to say:

> *In 2006, for example, subprime lenders pumped more than a billion dollars in to 22 Detroit Zip Codes.*
>
> *These were not the old 30-year fixed-rate mortgages invented in the New Deal. On the contrary, a high proportion were adjustable-rate mortgages—in other words, the interest rate would vary according to changes in short-term lending rates. Many were also interest-only mortgages, without amortization (repayment of principal), even when the principal represented 100 percent of the assessed value of the mortgage property. And most had introductory "teaser" periods, whereby the initial interest payments—usually for the first two years—were kept artificially low, with the cost of the loan backloaded . . .*
>
> *In Detroit, only a minority of these loans were going to first-time homebuyers. They were nearly all refinancing deals, which allowed borrowers to treat their homes as cash machines, converting their existing equity into cash and using the proceeds to pay off credit-card debts, carry out renovations, or buy new consumer durables.*

As Ferguson points out in his article, *"subprime lending worked beautifully— as long, that is, as interest rates stayed low, people kept their jobs, and real-estate prices continued to rise."*

Now replicate millions of times over, across the entire United States, what was going on in Detroit with respect to people unwittingly or otherwise miring themselves in subprime mortgages. Housing prices had been rising

10 per cent, 15 percent and sometimes more for years while average annual wages remained flat. What self-respecting economist, let alone the entire Federal Reserve—which employs hundreds of economists, many with PhDs after their names—could not figure this one out?

> **Instead of relying on their computer models and traditional beliefs in how economies and the markets work, common sense should have kicked in.**

Instead of relying on their computer models and traditional beliefs in how economies and the markets work, common sense should have kicked in. They should have at least understood that a storm was brewing and taken some steps to determine what was at risk, what they could do to avoid or at least reduce the impact of the storm and how they would handle any potential crisis, should one arise. And arise, one did!

Aha!

In their abandonment of seeking out common sense warning signs and solutions, they subsequently eroded the public trust in government oversight and the Federal Reserve's reputation, or brand.

In fact, in the wake of this financial debacle the brands of nearly every major financial institution, the agencies that rate these institutions' financial products, as well as Fannie Mae, Freddie Mac, the Securities and Exchange Commission (SEC) and other government regulatory agencies were shattered, to the point where some companies went completely out of business, or were forced into mergers, were restructured or otherwise lost public trust.

The saddest part to this story is that the fiduciary responsibilities our financial institutions failed to meet, and the oversight responsibilities many of our government agencies failed to enforce, were relied upon by millions of Americans, many of whom unwittingly got caught up in the Great Recession of our time. And all for the want of a bit of common sense and a true understanding of what a good brand is supposed to represent and adhere to—honesty and trust!

"Let's give this some thought"

Questions to initiate and stimulate staff and board discussions

- Are we stuck in the ways in which we think?

- Are we so reliant on our computer models and other technologies that we've abandoned commonsense solutions?

- Do we see the big picture, or do we have our heads in the sand?

- Are we willing to sacrifice our organization's brand, or reputation, because of our unwillingness to face the brutal facts?

Aha! Moment #12

Exercise Due Diligence

"I observe the physician with the same diligence as the disease."

John Donne
British poet

Aha! Moment #12

Exercise Due Diligence

The World is Not Always What It Appears to be

As we have so painfully—and so often—experienced, the world is not always what it appears to be.

Many years ago, when my sons were very young, my wife and I would read to them every night before they went to bed. One evening my wife was out attending a class for her graduate degree and I was home alone with the boys. Our oldest, Brian, who was nearly five years old at the time, asked me to read from the children's classic *The Story of Babar,* the tale about a young elephant who witnesses the grizzly death of his beloved mother and ends up leaving the jungle and journeying to Paris. It was a book the boys loved, and one my wife and I often read to them at their request.

After I finished reading to them, I sent the boys off to brush their teeth, and through the bathroom door I overheard the following:

"But I don't want to die," whimpered 3-year-old Peter.

"Oh, don't worry, Pete," Brian, said matter of factly. *"Dad's going to die first because he's the oldest, then Mom's going to die. You and me, Pete, we're going to live for a long time, and*

then I'm going to die because I'm older than you . . . Then you're going to die."

Through the bathroom door, which had been left ajar, I could hear Peter whimper, *"But I don't want to die."*

I felt my heart pound. My great hope is that the scenario Brian laid out for his disconsolate little brother plays out in real life. At the time, however, it struck me how Brian was exhibiting perfectly good sense—for a five-year-old. In a perfect world, that's the way things should play themselves out. It also occurred to me that at the ripe old age of 5, Brian was placing a great deal of trust in his beliefs. Small children trust that their parents will—and can—protect them from all evil and danger. Psychologists tell us that children who do not manifest such trust grow up emotionally damaged and are at a psychological disadvantage when it comes to extending their trust and love to others.

> **As an adult decision maker, sometimes a good dose of skepticism about others and the way the world works isn't such a bad thing.**

But as an adult decision maker, sometimes a good dose of skepticism about others and the way the world works isn't such a bad thing.

Remember Bernie Madoff?

On December 10, 2008, long-time Wall Street wizard Bernard Madoff summoned his sons to his posh New York City apartment, saying *"he wasn't sure he would be able to hold it together"* at the office, according to Securities and Exchange Commission documents.

Earlier that day, Madoff's sons reportedly had confronted their father when he told them he was ready to distribute annual bonuses to employees. They knew that their father's investment firm, which he had founded in 1960, was struggling to pay its investors an estimated $7 billion, which they had requested as part of a massive investor withdrawal from what was at the time a wildly gyrating stock market. Consequently, the sons asked their father how the firm could possibly pay bonuses when it could not meet the financial demands of its investors?

In response, Madoff revealed to his sons that he was *"finished,"* that the business was *"a giant Ponzi scheme . . . . all just one big lie,"* according to SEC documents. The sons subsequently reported their father to the authorities, and the following day Madoff was charged with stealing as much as $50 billion from those who entrusted their money—some, their entire life savings—to him. It is thought to be the largest fraud in the history of Wall Street, and perpetrated by a man who for decades was considered by many one of the Street's lions, a pioneer in electronic trading and a former chairman of NASDAQ.

Madoff was reputed to be a shy but friendly man who, whether the stock market went up or went down, managed to deliver steady, above-average annual returns to those who invested with him, including family, friends and friends of friends, as well as many charitable foundations. His company's Web site declared: *"Clients know that Bernard Madoff has a personal interest in maintaining the unblemished record of value, fair-dealing, and high ethical standards that has always been the firm's hallmark."*

But words are cheap, and unfortunately for Madoff's investors, it turned out that nothing he wrote on his website could have been further from the truth.

The Madoff scandal gives new meaning to the trite but true saying: If it's too good to be true, it probably is. It certainly reaffirms that the world often is not what it appears to be. Even *"smart money"* got burned by Madoff's Ponzi scheme because investors failed to exercise due diligence when it came to investing with him.

> Even *"smart money"* got burned by Madoff's Ponzi scheme because investors failed to exercise due diligence when it came to investing with him.

What is Due Diligence?

Due diligence is a legal term used mostly when one company has an interest in acquiring another. It implies a diligent effort on the part of the company making the acquisition to fully understand all the obligations of the company it intends to purchase, including its debts, pending and potential lawsuits, leases, warranties, long-term customer agreements, employment contracts, distribution agreements, compensation arrangements, and more.

Due diligence should be a part of every significant decision a person or an organization makes.

But when it comes to personal and organizational decision-making, due diligence should go beyond mergers and acquisitions and be a part of every significant decision a person or an organization makes.

Aha!

Caveat emptor! Buyer beware! Meaning that nothing should be taken at face value, even the reputation of others you choose to associate with, regardless of their perceived reputations.

Co-branding: You're Judged by the Company You Keep

As a communications consultant, for example, I always caution clients to exercise due diligence whenever they are considering entering into a co-branding relationship with another organization or company.

Many professional communicators and marketers promote co-branding as an opportunity to create marketing synergy by placing their client's brand name or logo in conjunction with the brand name or logo of like-minded or complementary organizations or companies. Think of the *Intel Inside* sticker that many personal computer companies put on their products or how most fundraising events display the names of major sponsors on banners and in event promotional materials.

Co-branding also applies to the opportunity of displaying multiple brand names or corporate logos on a single Web site, so that people who visit the site see it as a joint enterprise.

From my point of view, however, co-branding is more than placing your *logo* beside that of another organization's or company's; co-branding is placing your <u>reputation</u> alongside that of another's.

My mother always told me *"You're judged by the company you keep."* So, be sure to use due diligence before entering into any kind of co-branding relationship.

> **Co-branding is more than placing your *logo* beside that of another organization's or company's; co-branding is placing your <u>reputation</u> alongside that of another's.**

At the very least, the reputations of the companies and organizations you co-brand with should be equal, if not superior, to your own.

"Let's give this some thought"

Questions to initiate and stimulate staff and board discussions

- Are we always aware of the environment in which we are doing business, the people we are doing business with and the impact they can have on our brand?

- Do we readily place our brand along side that of another company or organization without first doing our due diligence to learn more about them?

- What systems can we put in place to ensure our brand is always protected before we get into a co-branding situation?

- Do we have a tendency to be star-struck or flattered whenever a larger, better branded company wants to co-brand or do business with us?

Aha! Moment #13

A Good Brand is Dynamic, Not Static

"A product can be quickly outdated, but a successful brand is timeless."

Stephen King
Advertising Professional

A Good Brand is Dynamic, Not Static

Here Today . . .

We are living in an age of paradigm shifts where traditional ways of thinking and doing business don't always hold up. Innovation is moving at an unimaginable pace.

As a self-employed communications consultant, for years I depended on snail mail and courier services to deliver my written materials to clients. The modus operandi, or MO, I employed at the time was to allow two hours for the courier to pick up the package from my home office and another two hours to get it to a local client—barring any heavy traffic or bad weather, that is, which could of course easily extend the time at either end.

Once the package was picked up, I would follow up with a phone call to the client to ensure them that the package was on its way and for them to check with their receptionist or front desk at about the time it was scheduled to arrive so that it wouldn't get misplaced or lost at their end. Despite the $20 to $50 average fee per delivered package (which usually got billed back to the client), at the time I thought this was a pretty efficient process.

Then came the fax machine.

What used to take a minimum of half a workday or more by courier could now be accomplished in minutes. I bought my first fax in the mid 1980s. Forget that I paid about $1,200 for it and that every now and then it would jam or run out of paper when I wasn't around to install a fresh roll. To me, the fax machine represented the end of history as I knew it. It was magic. Simply dial up the client's fax number, run the pages through the machine and, voila, in practically no time at all my written words magically appeared on a similar machine in my client's office. The deed was done for the cost of a phone call. No muss, no fuss. No worrying about traffic or bad weather to hold things up. What could be simpler, cheaper or more efficient?

> **To me, the fax machine represented the end of history as I knew it. It was magic.**

Who could have ever imagined email, which to my kids is now Jurassic, given the advent of FaceBook and other social networking opportunities?

And the experts tell us that we're only at the cusp of the technological revolution!

It's only getting faster

Consider this:

> It has been observed . . . that if the last 50,000 years of man's existence were divided into lifetimes of approximately sixty-two years each, there have been about 800 such lifetimes. Of these 800, fully 650 were spent in caves.
>
> Only during the last 70 lifetimes has it been possible to communicate effectively from one lifetime to another—as writing made it possible to do. Only during the last six lifetimes did masses of men ever see a printed word. Only during the last four has it been possible to measure time with any precision. Only in the last two has anyone anywhere used an electric motor. And the overwhelming majority of all the

> *material goods we use in daily life today have been developed*
> *within the present, the 800th, lifetime.*

The above is an excerpt from Alvin Toffler's popular book, *Future Shock*—which was first published in 1971. I doubt back then that even Mr. Toffler, a renowned futurist, could have imagined the exponential pace that technological advances would acquire in such a short period of time.

It would be only five years from the publication of *Future Shock* before Steve Wozniak and Steve Jobs formed the Apple Computer Company and began to sell personal computers, also known as microcomputers. At first used mostly by techie types, personal computers quickly caught the imagination of the general public. Now ubiquitous—it's hard to find a desktop that doesn't sport one—they have revolutionized the way we communicate and do business. If not fused to our hips, they have evolved to the point that many of them now can be found on our laps. But much more was—and is—yet to come.

Before the 1980s, something called ARPANET (Advanced Research Projects Agency Net)—which would soon morph into what we know today as the internet—was known only to people in the department of defense and a handful of academicians, who developed and used this unique network of mainframe computers primarily for military defense purposes.

It wasn't until the 1990s that the Internet would become part of our popular culture and change the world more radically than few, if any, inventions before it, arguably even more radically than the personal computer. Today, there is hardly a place on the planet where people cannot instantly connect with practically anyone. Marshall McLuhan's global village has become a reality. Not only can people connect to one another more easily than in any other time in history; suddenly generations of man's accumulated knowledge is at our fingertips.

> **Not only can people connect to one another more easily than in any other time in history; suddenly generations of man's accumulated knowledge is at our fingertips.**

So how does all this revert back to an Aha! moment in brand management?

Organizations, and those who lead them, need to be increasingly vigilant and open to change and its impact on how they perceive, conduct and adapt their businesses to the brave new world we've entered. It's no longer acceptable to rely on ideological beliefs that more often than not will be unable to stand the test of time, which is forever becoming more and more compressed by technology.

I'm not suggesting we put all of our eggs in the high-tech basket for the answers to our organizational and operational challenges, either. On the contrary. If anything, I believe it's incumbent upon us to exhibit a bit of circumspection about all the communication technology at our fingertips.

When it comes to brand, I'm particularly referring to all the social media so many of us seem so enamored with. As I warn my clients, *"Good news travels fast; bad news travels faster."* So be certain that all

"Good news travels fast; bad news travels faster."

the news that circulates over the Internet about your company is true and accurate.

Also, let's not confuse information with wisdom. Google the word "technology" and in 0.22 seconds you have more than 1 billion sites to choose from. No one is able to connect all the dots generated by all this information to give it perspective, context and meaning, let alone wisdom. And if there were such a person, whose perspective, context, meaning and wisdom would it represent, anyway?

"Let's give this some thought"

Questions to initiate and stimulate staff and board discussions

- Are we aware of and sensitive to the impact technology can have on our brand?

- In this age of social media are we aware of what others are saying about us and what effect it may be having on our brand?

- How can we use technology to better manage our brand?

- If we do not take full advantage of technology, what competitive advantage do we lose?

Aha! Moment #14

Accept the New Normal

> *"You have to accept whatever comes and the only important thing is that you meet it with courage and with the best that you have to give."*
>
> Eleanor Roosevelt
> First Lady

Accept the New Normal

As an excuse not to change or do something differently, how often have you heard someone in your organization say, "Well . . . this is the way we've always done it!"

Don't Get Stuck

Again, this is no time to be an ideologue, or in other words, to be stuck in your old habits and ways.

> **We have entered into the Age of the New Normal.**

Partly due to the Great Recession, partly due to rapid advances in technology and partly due to changes in our cultural norms we have entered into what I refer to as the Age of the New Normal. And this New Normal is affecting every facet of how organizations conduct their businesses, from raising funds to using new technologies to workplace issues.

To stay current and maintain a viable brand as an organization in this Age of the New Normal, here are just a few of the questions that need answers:

How well do our employees work together?

The Age of the New Normal forces us to address the different work styles of aging Boomers versus young Millennials, or those born between 1978 and the early 1990s.

If you want to get the most out of your workforce, your organization needs to learn the differences between these two generations and how to leverage their respective strengths through training, setting clear goals and expectations, providing meaningful feedback, creating a flexible work environment and rewarding employees for their efforts.

This isn't always easy. For example, where Boomers prefer more "face time" and personal encounters in the workplace, Millennials are perfectly happy to communicate via email and other techno-based virtual methods, and want more flexibility to work from home.

> **Where Boomers prefer more "face time" and personal encounters in the workplace, Millennials are perfectly happy to communicate via email.**

For Boomers to tell Millennials, "But this is the way we've always done it" isn't necessarily going to make for a healthy workplace environment.

If your organization is a nonprofit, below are a few additional questions you need to ask . . .

How dependent are we on government funding?

For decades, countless nonprofits have relied largely or exclusively on local, state and federal funding, or a combination of all three, to achieve their missions. If yours is one of them, and you haven't already experienced a decrease in your funding, brace yourself. Given the state of most government budgets, it's just a matter of time.

> **The Age of the New Normal demands that you start seeking alternate sources of funding.**

The Age of the New Normal demands that you start seeking alternate sources of funding. Despite these hard economic times, there is money to tap into. Which leads us to the next question . . . .

Do we still believe that marketing and branding would make us look too much like the for-profit sector?
If so, get over it!

A lot of the available non-government money that's out there is in the hands of people who made their fortunes in the private sector. Many are seeking to support good causes. But only organizations that can effectively and clearly make their case by successfully explaining to these potential funders who they are, what they do, how they do it—and most important, why it matters—will be on the receiving end.

In other words, marketing and branding should be integral parts of your business strategy.

Are we still trying to raise money under the rubric of being a "charity that makes a difference"?
If so, you've got a tough row to hoe.

Under the New Normal, funders are seeking ever-greater accountability, transparency, responsibility—and demonstrated outcomes.

> **Under the New Normal, funders are seeking ever-greater accountability, transparency, responsibility—and demonstrated outcomes.**

To simply say you make a difference will no longer cut the mustard. You need to show how you make that difference. And the more data you have to support your claims, the better.

Which leads us to . . .

How well do we collect and leverage our data?

A lot of nonprofits don't even bother to collect data, and those that do often don't use the data in a way to help promote their organization's narrative or story.

The New Normal says it's not enough to tell prospective funders how many people walked through your doors last year. The New Normal wants to know, among other things, how your services improved the lives of these people, what these people are doing now and what impact your work has on the community at large.

Are we getting the most out of our volunteers?

Similar to issues revolving around Boomers versus Millennials, we've entered a New Normal for volunteerism, as well.

Studies have shown that the majority of today's volunteers, regardless of whether they are young or old, are seeking meaningful volunteer experiences that take greater advantage of their skills, give them more responsibility and provide greater flexibility with respect to when they can volunteer.

Many are seeking more on-line volunteer opportunities. Some want to volunteer as a family unit, while still others say that they want the organizations to which they give their time to get to know them better, especially when it comes to being more sensitive to gender, culture, language and age differences.

And here's a final thought: If a Millennial comes to you with an idea about technology, or anything else for that matter, do not respond by saying, "But that's not the way we've done it in the past."

Instead, you might want to ask, "How can we use your idea to improve our brand?"

> **If a Millennial comes to you with an idea about technology, or anything else for that matter, do not respond by saying, "But that's not the way we've done it in the past."**

Yes, listening is part of the New Normal, as well.

"Let's give this some thought"

Questions to initiate and stimulate staff and board discussions

- How well are we dealing with intergenerational issues?

- Do we truly understand what motivates Millennials versus Baby Boomers?

If your organization is a nonprofit:

- Are we still heavily reliant on government funding? If so, what do we need to do to diversify our revenue streams?

- Are we devoting any of our resources to marketing and branding?

- Do we have any systems in place for getting our brand messages to our target audiences? If not, why not?

- Are we accountable, transparent and responsible? And do we demonstrate outcomes?

- Do we collect appropriate data? And if so, are we using it to tell our brand story?

- Do we understand the needs and desires of today's volunteers, and are we working to fulfill those needs?

Aha! Moment #15

Keep Your Eye on the Ball

"The difference between men and women is that, if given the choice of saving the life of an infant or catching a fly ball, a woman will automatically choose to save the life of the infant, without even considering if there's a man on base."

Dave Barry
American humorist

Keep Your Eye on the Ball

Have We Gone Daft?!

On March 8, 2008, The Washington Post ran a story on the front page of its Metro section about Michael Holland—a mentally disabled father of four and loyal 18-year employee with Safeway—who, while on his way to a short work break, failed to pay for a glazed doughnut and a small carton of milk. Total value: $1.78. It turned out to be a bad employee decision.

Holland claimed that he had all good intentions of paying for what he took. Regardless, the company reportedly suspended him, ordered him to pay for the food—plus a $50 fine—and then fired him. Which turned out to be an even worse employer decision.

Company officials said they were simply applying Safeway's "zero tolerance" policy against employee theft. Under pressure from Holland's union—not to mention the media glare—Safeway later reinstated Holland.

Employee anti-theft clauses, and the need to rigorously enforce them as part of corporate policy, make complete sense. Companies would go bust if workers felt free to simply help themselves to whatever the company produced or sold without some form of retribution.

However, when it comes to corporate policy and governance what does not make sense, at least to me, is that about the same time Mr. Holland walked off with his $1.78 worth of donut and milk:

- The former CEOs of Merrill Lynch and Countrywide Mortgage—after years of bad decision-making that led their companies to lose billions—jumped out of their respective planes with board-approved golden parachutes worth hundreds of millions of dollars.

- The former CEO's and senior officers of government-sponsored enterprises (GSEs) Fannie Mae and Freddie Mac, the nation's secondary mortgage market giants—both of which were suspected of fudging their books to trigger exorbitant executive bonuses—blithely scampered off with hundreds of millions of dollars they insisted they had coming to them.

- Wall Street executives—while they were devising financial instruments that it turns out they themselves didn't understand, and that helped create the financial mess that we're in now—saw fit to award themselves more than $160 billion—in BONUSES—from 2002-2008. That's on top of their annual high six and seven figure salaries.

In hindsight, common sense should tell us that corporate America was looking through the wrong end of the telescope. It should have been focusing more on the business decisions that were taking place in its executive offices and boardrooms than on penny-ante employee theft.

> **Corporate America was looking through the wrong end of the telescope.**

Think of the U.S. automotive industry's penchant for building monstrous SUVs while Toyota and Honda were cornering the market with their gas-saving hybrids. Or the sub-prime mortgage industry that freely doled out specious loan products to people it had identified as high-risk borrowers without documenting their incomes or job histories. Where was the common sense? Who was providing brand management oversight regarding these corporate decisions?

By the fall of 2008, many of America's top corporate executives—identified and compensated for ostensibly being the best and brightest among us—brought the United States face to face with its worst economic crisis since the Great Depression. As a result of years of their making decisions that flew in the face of common sense, millions of Americans are losing their homes, jobs, pensions, health insurance and more.

Now, how many Michael Holland incidences would it have taken for that to happen!

What's That You Say?

"As officers and employees of Enron Corp., its subsidiaries, and its affiliated companies, we are responsible for conducting the business affairs of the companies in accordance with all applicable laws and in a moral and honest manner."

These are the words of Kenneth Lay, former chairman and CEO of the now defunct Enron Corp. Enron's 64-page *Code of Ethics* went on to reflect policies approved by the company's board of directors and a company that at one time enjoyed a reputation for being fair and honest, and highly respected. Enron's ethics code specified that *"An employee shall not conduct himself or herself in a manner which directly or indirectly would be detrimental to the best interests of the Company or in a manner which would bring to the employee financial gain separately derived as a direct consequence of his or her employment with the Company."*

Aha!

Well, we all know how that turned out! What else needs to be said?

"Let's give this some thought"

Questions to initiate and stimulate staff and board discussions

- Do we have our eye on the ball? Meaning, do we know what's important when it comes to our business, and how to address both employee and management issues when it seems things are starting to go wrong, or getting out of hand?

- When we create policy or a code of ethics for our company or organization, do we adhere to them or are we just paying lip service?

- Do we hold everyone, from our support staff to our board members, accountable and responsible for their actions, decisions and behaviors?

- How much do we value our brand and how much are we willing to protect it from becoming just so much bull?

Endnotes

I disclosed at the very outset that this book was written as much out of personal frustration and disappointment as anything else. For me, it's more than disappointing not to be able to trust the very institutions we were taught to value and respect. It leaves me feeling very uncomfortable and uneasy, and I imagine you might feel the same.

What follows is the manifestation of some of my frustration in the form of commentary aired on WAMU radio, NPR's affiliate in Washington, DC, on November 17, 2009, near the height of the Great Recession. The following transcript of that commentary summarizes my frustration—and a lot of what this book is about.

Announcer:
Commentator Larry Checco says it may be easier to follow Ralph Waldo Emerson's advice to "trust thyself" than it is to trust anyone else.

Commentary:
"No more bull."

That has become my personal rallying cry against corporations, organizations and institutions that have violated my trust. And I don't think I'm alone.

Question*: What happened when the once-venerable Merrill Lynch invested more time, energy and money creating and widely marketing its logo—that bold, aggressive-looking, high-profile bull—than it did focusing on being a good steward of its investors' money?*

Answer: *No more bull!*

Merrill Lynch is an easy and graphic target of a once well-known, recognizable and respected corporate brand gone bust.

But the same thing has happened to numerous other companies and organizations we once trusted with our finances and our livelihoods, including household names such as Arthur Anderson, Enron, General Motors, Chrysler, Lehman Brothers, Bear Stearns, Fannie Mae and Freddie Mac, just to name a few.

Dare I say that even some of our religious institutions, and their leaders, have failed us miserably?

"Who Do You Trust?" was the name of an entertaining 1950s TV game show. Now it's a question we must seriously ask ourselves every day.

We can't trust our government to succeed in looking after our best interests: Think of the Securities and Exchange Commission (SEC) and Federal Emergency Management Agency, better known as FEMA.

And many of our politicians, pundits and pastors have violated our trust with their hypocrisy, immorality and horrendously unethical behavior.

As for the financial mayhem created by some on Wall Street, I say instead of bonuses, let's force them to live on minimum wage until they figure out how to replace the seven million jobs lost by their greedy and poor high-risk, if not sometimes illegal decision making, resulting in trickle-down misery for countless millions of Americans.

A recent Business Week article titled "The Great Trust Offensive" described how companies as diverse as McDonald's, Ford and American Express are changing their marketing to restore what it calls "that most valuable of corporate assets."

Sorry, guys. You had your shot with those multi-million dollar ad campaigns that encouraged us to believe that "Quality is Job 1" and that we could "Invest with Confidence". You created expectations you couldn't meet—and we're just not buying it anymore.

In case you're still in denial, this is no longer business as usual.

If you want our trust back you're going to have to earn it—the old fashioned way—by being transparent, accountable and responsible; by understanding your place in our society and how much your decision-making not only affects your bottom line, but ours, as well.

You're going to have to learn to be better corporate citizens and spiritual and political leaders—not by paying lip service, but by living up to the values you publicly espouse through your marketing, press releases and preaching.

And that's no bull!

Finally
It's sad to realize that not much has changed in the years since Enron's collapse or the above commentary was aired. Believing that our once most venerated corporations and institutions will change for the better on their own is the triumph of hope over experience. But we get absolutely nowhere if as managers and leaders of organizations we don't at least identify the pitfalls many of our companies and organizations can fall into—and some never find their way out.

My hope is that this book has helped in some small way to bring awareness to many of the pitfalls your organization may be facing as it relates to its brand, and that *Aha! Moments in Brand Management* has inspired you to think about what needs to be done to resolve some of these issues—and what the consequences may be if you don't.

I leave you with one final thought: Without the people we employ, with all of their talents, skills, diversity—and, yes, faults—what we think of as organizations would be nothing more than soulless collections of bricks and mortar.

> **Your organization's brand is a referendum and reflection on how it treats its people.**

In many respects, your organization's brand is a referendum and reflection on how it treats its people. My experience working with many organizations over the years has taught me that the better its people are treated—including employees, customers, clients and volunteers—the better the organization's brand.

It's often that simple.

Acknowledgements

With a little help from my friends

Anyone who's ever spent serious time trying to put words on paper knows how isolating, and often frustrating, an experience it can be. Worse than writer's block and bouts of despair ("Why did I ever start this project?!"), we often find ourselves trapped in "loops," or thought patterns from which we can't seem to escape.

Stepping away from the computer and taking a brisk walk around the block often help to bring new and fresh thoughts to mind. But sometimes it takes more than that. Sometimes it takes the ideas, opinions, critical eyes and encouragement of those whose friendship, judgment and professionalism you trust and respect. And I am fortunate to have many who fall into that category.

My profoundest thanks go to my wife, Laurie, whose love and encouragement over the course of our more than 30 years of marriage has been the sustenance of my career as a writer and consultant. I could not do what I do without her. I tease her when I say she's the luckiest woman in the world when I know it's I who is the luckiest man. And to my sons, Brian and Peter, for whom I hope life holds countless positive *"Aha!"* moments.

To my good friend Peter Shann Ford, who tirelessly nagged me to write this book. *"Texada!"*

When I got trapped in my "loops," many others helped me to escape and take a different tack. They include many good friends and professional colleagues: Darrell Blandford, Arthur Bruno, Steve Casady, Jack Detzner,

David Homorody, Jeff Finn, Gail Fiorelli, Roland Fiorelli, Joanne Fritz, Jason Hall, Jocelyn Harmon, Michael Lesparre, Doug Lipton, Vicki Meade, Jake Plante, Lynn Rodman, Barbara Stob, Ken Terrell and Bill Weger.

And then there are those too numerous to mention, namely the scores of organizations and thousands of people I have worked for and with over my 30-year career, those who have taken my courses and others who have heard me speak at conferences and other venues around the country. It's been a wonderful career—and life—learning from and exchanging ideas with all of you.

Thank you!

About the Author

Larry Checco is president of Checco Communications and a nationally sought-after speaker on branding and leadership. He also serves as a consultant to both large and small organizations, companies, foundations and government agencies. In addition, Larry conducts courses and workshops, and is a faculty member of the NeighborWorks® Training Institute—an adjunct of Southern New Hampshire University.

In addition to selling thousands of copies throughout the United States, Larry's first book, **Branding for Success: A Roadmap for Raising the Visibility and Value of Your Nonprofit Organization**, has found success in Australia, Canada, South Africa, Sweden, Israel, Southeast Asia and elsewhere around the globe. He has been recognized as a leading branding professional by Brand Gurus (www.brandgurus.net), and his articles on branding are cited and reprinted on countless websites.

Larry holds a degree in Economics from Syracuse University, as well as an MA in Journalism and Public Affairs from American University. He lives in Silver Spring, MD, with his wife, Laurie, and sons, Brian and Peter.

To learn more about this book, Larry and how to engage his consulting services log onto www.checcocommunications.net